THE NATIONAL POETRY SERIES

was established in 1978 to ensure the publication of five poetry books annually through five participating publishers. Publication is funded by the Lannan Foundation; Stephen Graham; Joyce & Seward Johnson Foundation; Glenn and Renee Schaeffer, Juliet Lea Hillman Simmonds Foundation; Tiny Tiger Foundation; and Charles B. Wright III.

THE WINNERS OF THE 2008 OPEN COMPETITION
Anna Journey of Houston, Texas, *If Birds Gather Your Hair for Nesting*
Chosen by Thomas Lux, to be published by University of Georgia Press

Douglas Kearney of Van Nuys, California, *The Black Automaton* }
Chosen by Catherine Wagner, to be published by Fence Books }

Adrian Matejka of Edwardsville, Illinois, *Mixology*
Chosen by Kevin Young, to be published by Penguin Books

Kristin Naca of Minneapolis, Minnesota, *Bird Eating Bird*
Chosen by Yusef Komunyakaa for The National Poetry Series mtvU Prize,
to be published by HarperCollins Publishers

Sarah O'Brien of Brookfield, Ohio, *catch light*
Chosen by David Shapiro, to be published by Coffee House Press

CATHERINE WAGNER ON THE BLACK AUTOMATON

First, you have to see Douglas Kearney's visual poems, which cheekily diagram cultural memes as if they were parts of speech (as they are). *The Black Automaton* has its share of sharp, tender lyrics, too; like the visual pages, these exploit the political possibilities of puns and the way meanings hinge on inexact resemblance. Kearney's poems tweak and skewer pop culture and literary sources from Paul Laurence Dunbar to T. S. Eliot to traditional ballads and blues (see Kearney's ruthless version of some lines from "Prufrock"). Jokes like "IT beeze W. E. B. dubious" are brutally funny, and throughout, the wordplay spins hard arguments: if "to look away, look away is to be a 'ninny" (racially charged words hover off the page), "to look, to look is to be a massachist." That is: how to proceed when the options—looking away from reality and looking at it—both pretty much suck? It's when the searchlights hit us that "new eyes glare back"—watch out, put on your hardhat, because we're under construction from the outside in—in the furnace of Los Angeles in 1992 and everywhere else. Kearney's work turns poetic and cultural conventions disquietingly inside out.

Catherine Wagner is the author of My New Job, Macular Hole *and* Miss America.

THE BLACK AUTOMATON

THE BLACK

©2009, 2011 ————————————————————————————————————

all rights reserved

designed by ————————————————————————————

text set in ITC New Baskerville; titles set in ITC Franklin Gothic

published in the United States by ——————————————————

Science Library 320
University at Albany
1400 Washington Avenue
Albany, NY 12222
www.fenceportal.org

are distributed by Consortium Book Sales and Distribution www.cbsd.com
and printed in Canada by Printcrafters www.printcraftersinc.com

Library of Congress cataloguing in publication data Kearney, Douglas [1974–]

The Black Automaton/Douglas Kearney

Library of Congress control number: 2009932511

ISBN   1-934200-28-5 }
ISBN 13 978-1-934200-28-5 } *first edition* 4 5 6 7 8 9 10

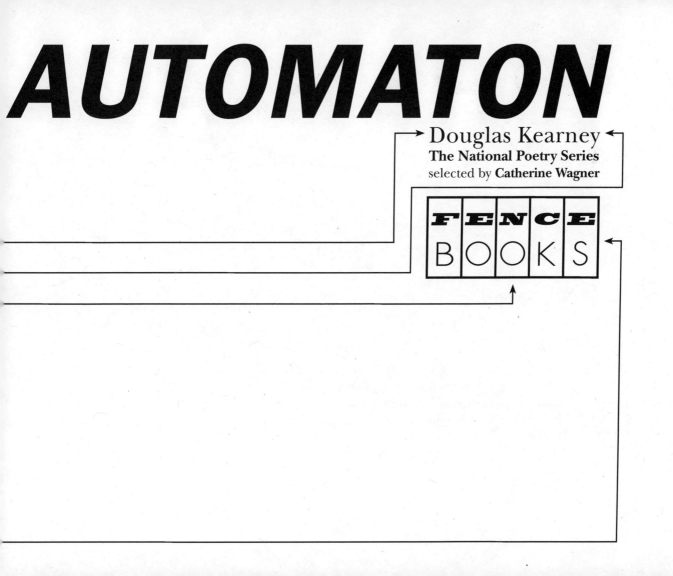

AUTOMATON

Douglas Kearney

The National Poetry Series

selected by **Catherine Wagner**

FENCE BOOKS

TABLE OF CONTENTS

for Nicole,
because you fought for it.

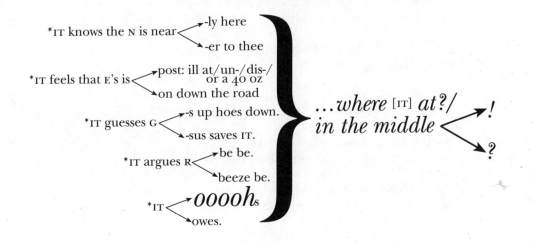

*IT knows the N is near— -ly here / -er to thee

*IT feels that E's is— post: ill at/un-/dis-/ or a 40 OZ / on down the road

*IT guesses G— -s up hoes down. / -sus saves IT.

*IT argues R— be be. / beeze be.

*IT— *ooooh*s / owes.

} ...*where* [IT] *at?*/ *in the middle* — ! / ?

RADIO

the first black you met was on the radio.
this is true even if you lived with blacks.

the first black to speak the word *radio*
knew it meant the same as *blood*.

the first black to know *blood* meant *radio*,
claimed *radio* meant *love*, to better lure you.

the first black you dreamed about was on the radio
and waited for you there each night to fuck you,

you still believe this and sleep with the radio
on or off; it all depends.

the first blacks to realize they were *blacks* became radios
at once, singing something that could never be english.

the first black to confess it was a radio
did so to account for the snow filling its voice.

the first black you heard was a radio
and did not speak english even if it did: radios cannot speak.

the first blacks to change *radio*'s
meaning from *love* back to *blood* are still here

and want to fuck you. they are doing so on the radio
right now. you don't like it but go to sleep.

TALLAHATCHIE LULLABYE, BABY

cattail cast tattles Till tale,
lowing low along the hollow.
crickets chirrup and ribbits lick-up.
what's chucked the 'hatchie swallow.

skin scow skiffs upon pond scum skin
going slow along the hollow.
now may mayfly alight brown brow.
what's chucked the 'hatchie swallow.

maybe bye baby bye baby by and by—
lowing low along the hollow—
we will slip the knot not slip will we?
what's chucked the 'hatchie swallow.

who's a bruise to blue hue 'hatchie,
going slow along the hollow?
who's a bruise to whose hue, 'hatchie?
what's chucked the 'hatchie swallow.

Kodak flash tattles Till tale
going slow among the hollow.
who's a bruise to bruise hue?
swallow what the 'hatchie chucks.

—Emmett Till (1941–1955)

THE BLACK AUTOMATON IN DE DESPAIR UB EXISTENCE #3: HOW CAN I BE DOWN?

IT won't just look away, look away.

another place./ ... another land.

IT beeze W. E. B. dubious: ——————
e.g. can't get groan sans busted cherry.
choke

{the simple back and forth,
the same/old ...

keeping one eye open { to look away, look away is to be
just clocking { a 'ninny. to look, to look is to be
a massachist.

or not
knot Toby

IT knows the world
is round whether it likes IT or not.
IT axes the first question:

(and then all the crows, circling.)

{all that
hurts [IT]. */let* [IT] *understand ...*

you wouldn't.
you won't.
you.

THE VOLTRON COMMUNIQUÉS

PAST THE PARAPET, FLURRIES, FEW STARS. ROUNDS EXPLODE ON DISTANT ROCKETS.

ATTN: BLACK LION
HNIC you, hunkered in the tower's
shadow, a rook passing for king. roar
yourself pale on how shit should be
in your would be. you seem
to figure you're the brains of this operation—
heart, too—would lop your hands
as proof, your sword a blazing light
flip-flopping to a damp planet.

when you change,
there's a face in your mouth. you're a circus act gone wrong.

> *the mouth in my mouth never says*
> *nothing ever. brothers, sisters; you might say*
> *I ate Dunbar's mask.*
> which got you
> what
> exactly?

you are here because a million people holler.
fool, there's always terror
in space, black as your scrap yard animal armor.
monsters are coming to tear you into yourself. black lion,
take that key out your chest. the screaming wind
on your back bumrushes you
off your pedestal. see how it lifts your foes, too.

LAPILLI FLARE TOWARD A FROSTY PASTURE. WARHEADS OVER URBAN LIGHTS.

BRO. RED LION:
what you lack in patience
you make up in kerosene.

every time your work is done,
cities are sooty skeletons.
but none of those are your bones;
you're only cogs, screws and fuel.
after they built you, they buried you
in the smoldering earth,
like a myth.
                there is always
                a they,
a fist of ashes thrown
into your eyes to make you blind
as animals, your jaws frothing.
but you're no animal; you're a machine.
and your mouth? cinder-filled. when a shop burns
like a church, it's not a church.
that's what you mean?

                I move and don't live.
                what made me?

when you light their cities, you are awake.
it's with dwindling smoke that you go back
down the hole to consider hell a kind of flesh.

EVERGREEN TREE LINE, DUSK STILL EARLY. STEEL HIND CLAWS TRAILING INTO FLAMES.

GREEN LION
green cat, green cat, why you lying?
where were you sleeping?
in a pine, a tycoon in green satin.

if you roar out there, alone, who hears?
only those nature things flittering
to your glittering metal fingers.

there's fighting to be fought, we could use an extra fist.
fighting in the stone-faced cities beyond your forest,
your people, crowded in alleys; no flowers to molest.

> *the elm and maple, doe and clover,*
> *the hart knows love when a hunter*
> *stares an x into its shoulder.*

when you croak in your straitjacket of oak and cedar,
will you wish to have known the hue of your own brother's
blood? what that color would do to your arbor?

SIDEWINDERS SEARCH MOUSE BURROWS FOR PUPS. BARREN RAVINE, THE DOWSING CRAFT.

DEAR YELLOW LION,
tell me about thirst.

no.

tell me
        about
                your thirst.

morning comes, you wake up
and the sun's fat, white hand slaps
your yellow hide.

morningtime, you rise,
and the sun smacks
the gold off your back.

I wonder what you wouldn't do to drink.

day breaks, you wake,
million insults of sand
work into your insides.

each daytime you rise
what now? still mad? no offense!
into your running engine.

how much wouldn't you do for a drink?

> *to befriend thirst, you must*
> *make an enemy of water.*

so, teach me about your thirst,
gold lion. break it down
before we drown.

IRIDESCENT FRY, STILL, IN THE DEEP WATER. STARS ALONE IN THE SKY.

TO: BLUE LION
distorted and slow, airless
and mute as a trout. the fish
have learned to eat everything but you—
            there's still time.

> RE: YOUR LACK OF COMMITMENT
> TO CONSISTENT VIGILANCE,
> YOU'VE CLEARLY LOST INTEREST IN RESISTANCE.

a lake is no place for a cat like you. at least
a river, or a sea floor of coral tenements.
at least a delta.

> *I said 'I will* not *be repeating myself.'*

> RE: YOUR LACK OF ATTENDANCE,
> NO DOUBT YOUR BUSINESS
> WAS OTHER THAN US.

crawfish, crawfish all you like.

> RE: YOUR LACK OF PASSION
> FOR REVOLUTION, WE ARE CERTAIN
> YOU'VE BEEN SOMEONE ELSE AGAIN.

into the sack, you. now: play fish.

FROM VOLTRON

just   couldn't/   get   it
        together/   the   right   hand/
                        didn't   know/   we   had   no/
        legs   to   stand/   on   and   what
the/   left   hand was/   doing   keeping
hope/   lifting   ev'ry   heart/   in   the   wine
        of   the/   word   forgetting/   our   feet   lessed/   but
        marched   on/   and   not coming/ over
        the   head/ dreaming of   dream/   ing   of any
                means/ necessary   by   all/   means
                        we   fought/   the beautiful
        black/   power   and   we/
no   justiced   and   pointsed/   and
                        pledged/   til   we   were   in
peaces/   and   warring   pieces   / we   couldn't
        form/   ulate   our   bodies
        said *yes/*   *ashé*   *amen*   and/   our
        mouth   said/   .../
                                        ../

FINAL CALL'S ECHO DIMINISHES. DAWN SHRINKS SHADOWS FROM ALYSSUM.

"SPIT OUT ALL BITTERNESS"

swarthy poet, your mouth a beautiful something of homemade
brooms for darkish dirt in darkish rooms. you hock your spit,
work dirt into mud
to sling, mud to shape into beautiful somethings and useful:
spirituals slanging escape routes. piñatas
full of good medicine.
red tandoors buried deep and bullish. and above all useful,
with all the etcs. of suicide/uplift;
requisite beauty
of indelible tans
and rising, even from the briny these lava rocks.
even from blank graves
these painted ghosts. even from the burbs these barbecue smokes. this is good
work. above all, work that doesn't code shift
or sport permanents,
cravats; but rolls up its sleeves like those who basketball shoe,
cotton, orange, diamond, tobacco, java,
sweat to buy mother-tongue
off layaway. you who replay the way grandmama wore
her hair indigenously, folk funk of pots, tattoos
and songs your uncles hung out
like dirty laundry. dig them up and use them to beat your people
into new songs. righteous art is a rod.
rods are very useful.
photograph the gouges your men made. blow them up. zoom on
the welts the women dealt. use no firewater,
needles, crack, no opium.
do this in ghettoes, behind sweatlodges and mountaintop dojos.

but if you decide, at last, you must break through,
there are explorers out
to discover, listening for voices to lomax,
dialects to misinterpret and surfaces
for new flags and maps.
they seek porters for jungle idylls, guides with machetes
and hoodoo to help them escape Uncle Sam, the Son
of Sam, Columbus,
Columbine, Mandingo, Manzanar—all our history's
bright foundries of burning skin. if you choose to help them
lose their bulging baggage
in swarthy airports and drive them to where they feel at home,
know then who might call your work beautiful,
above all, useful.

THE BLACK AUTOMATON IN WHAT IT IS #2: HYPERTENSION IN EFFIZZECT

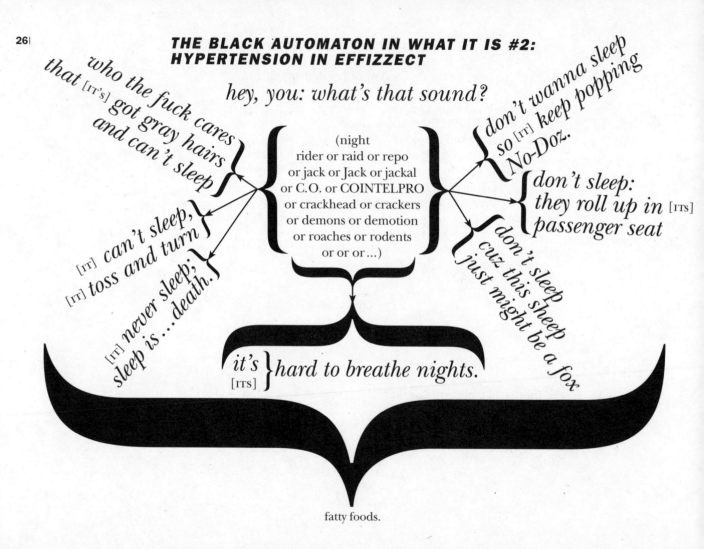

hey, you: what's that sound?

who the fuck cares
that [IT'S] got gray hairs
and can't sleep

[IT] can't sleep,
[IT] toss and turn

[IT] never sleep;
sleep is … death.

(night
rider or raid or repo
or jack or Jack or jackal
or C.O. or COINTELPRO
or crackhead or crackers
or demons or demotion
or roaches or rodents
or or or…)

don't wanna sleep
so [IT] keep popping
No-Doz.

don't sleep:
they roll up in [ITS]
passenger seat

don't sleep
cuz this sheep
just might be a fox

it's [ITS] } hard to breathe nights.

fatty foods.

MALIK CONSIDERS THE WINTER SEMESTER

                                  again,
I nuke the mug the U gave out
and water turns to heat.
the steam rises then falls
like it can't get out of bed. tonight,
the moon seems near unplugged.

I stare at the dull black sky
so long the water cools again.
the ramen still dry
in its package, it looks like hay
or maybe twine;
the microwave blinks *end*
where it should say the time.

            a ramen package says *shrimp*.
            another says *pork*.
            each something like what it says.

like I said I would, I kept the cards.
they're like paper gates that hinge, squeal
on my desk, by books I haven't read
and the tuneless radio.
                    the *congratulations*
in icy glitter. the *we're so proud*
in kente. the figure, water-colored brown
in cap and gown, to make me think
of me,

       the one with the Bearden
print, all angles and eyes,
a fragmented train,
the cut-out fields of brown
and black, they make me think—

SOMETIMES, I WALK TO THE BACK OF CAMPUS.
since winter hit, this shit's become a bit much.

first, the slush;
a few dark, lingering grits;
then everything white
like an empty pad on a desk of books.
I've wandered in and out of evenings,
a radio between stations, whispering
in night's ear, winter fields wondering
why I'm there.
              I watched the black grits
              disappear. everything white.

A SONG COMES CLEAR THROUGH THE RADIO,
it's nothing like me. then snow
fills the radio's throat.

my voicemail is nothing like me.
it doesn't know it's just the thing
that's there to be what's missing,

my family says it's nothing
like me,
           that's what the cards,
the free mug
help me see. that's why I'm here,
some starving, sweating pioneer
and why I stand in lecture
halls deciding how to disappear
                        more.

to leave the dorm, go past the fields,
frozen white. a lone, black bit of grit.
this is too much. the winter fields
and I wonder why I'm here.

        it didn't taste like shrimp, no.
        no, it didn't taste like pork.

                        IF I COULD
find the pieces of train in my mind,
paste them together, I would get a ticket,
take a dark seat and ride it to a station
free of these fields of snow.
                   it must be nearly time to go.
the phone rings like a conductor's bell,
I tell my voicemail our truth. I can't be
late. I already read what the microwave says.

and the fields and I wonder
why I'm here as December
calls its roll, the fields filled white
as a lecture hall. I take my seat.
I don't speak and yes, I am here. choked
as a radio between stations.

THE BLACK AUTOMATON IN DE DESPAIR UB EXISTENCE #1: UP YE MIGHTY RACE!!!

{ smack needle and wheedle
youngbleeds and biddies. *with everybody saying:*
swing down…/let me ride.

{ crack know shit—where TVs sit
and skeleton bricks. *who's that peeking in my window/pow!*
broken glass everywhere!

IT can't piss in a pot,

so the need is in a haystack.   /   so the lights have run off with the spoon.
looking for it is falling off a log.   coke is it and life is opening a can.

IT has a window to throw IT out of.

[IT] *can kiss the sky!*

up, up…

SHOWTIME IN THE BURNING CITY

THE WARM-UP ACT
the black smoke is hanging
there, a racy joke.
how do you tell the difference ..?
what do you get ..?
how many ..? million of em.

and right there is your problem.
can we all get—
like smoke, that guy. in the distance,
one could see the jokes
told loud into evening.

OPENING DUET

someone else's shit?
I mean, ain't but glass
between theirs and mine.

sell someone's shit?—
know damn well I will.
I'm between theirs, yours.

who you are is what you got.

I ask myself at the window
"who will I be today?" it's like

I'm already in,
checking who I was
before I got in

and I'm seeing who
I won't be when I'm back
outside of the glass.

who you can be is what you can get.

so yeah, it's someone else's shit.
now, do you want this shit or not?

THE RIOT ACT
what it is.   be.   look like.
          don't know   better
    ask somebody. scream!

I can't hear you!

everybody make some—
everybody in the house
          make some nooooise!

... over here!—everybody
          make some nooooise—
    ... over there!—I can't—

just a little bit louder.

say:

say:

said *say*:

a little bit louder.
I   can't   hear   you!

SONG FOR FOUR DANCERS

the four dancers move
like the blood on their feet is fire;
that man on the street,
a sweat-damp field.

THE RIOT. ACT II.
featuring chorus of blacks with candles

BLACK 1

angry enough to burn their house down.

BLACK 2

angry enough to burn my house down.

BLACK 3

angry enough to burn every house down.

diminuendo. garden grows, someone cracks
jokes, the chorus turns its head.
the freeway reels from the city
still ~~and~~ burning.

IT's a problem of semanthematics:
too many nothings. *zero, zero,*
zero, o'ed up

IT's a dismemory on an operating table:
awtopsy, auturvy. *... all* [ITS] *people*
eat chicken and watermelon

what [IT] look like

?

:

[IT] *ain't no real representative*
[IT] *ain't official*—[IT] *tentative*

IT's a rock that
jus keep rollin
downhill

ssssssssssss

so what [IT] *wanna do?*

shit.

how LA burned and hungry smoke licked
hot strokes
from the light-skimmed sky in my rearview
mirror.
revving hard, I found myself wanting
_____ Carlson,
a fine sister. she was a mezzo
sopran-
o. eager, I drove my gray beater
to her.
for choir, it was just a Wednesday.
it was
her mother came to the door: blue eyes
swollen
with News 5 and was she pale! *you should
go home—*
not like that! we got along: me, mom.
… not safe.
was it? "but there's choir"—I wanted
something
burning. sunset-bound from the Carlsons'
alone,
I wanted the yellow girl and flame
beating
from the car's ribcage. drove to the same
white church
where a blonde junior broke me into

nigger
when I was 8, remember her lips,
her teeth
white as church, white as _____ Carlson's mother,
white as
fire's starving heart. I wanted us
to loot
each other—sweet yellow girl and I,
no peace,
just to haul down the gilt drywall from
our frames,
claim nothing we needed, escaping,
raising
what I wanted over our shoulders,
our bits
of glass scattered, for neither of us
black-owned.

FISH HOOK LURE

it's 2000 and I am a writer
who gets paid
to write about fish hooks.

well, I get paid
to make you want
fish hooks.

on Monday, I will
scrub off my weekend
and put on clothing
that best suits
a fish hook lure.

then, I will punch
a car-sized hole
through the misty
beryl of autumn air.

I will smile
at my coworkers
in their ironed shirts,
and hope they weren't
too despicable
after their dutiful hours
in suburban churches.

perhaps they hope
the same about me,
unshaved and grinning
vacantly,

mind and mouth
full of fish hooks.

CITY WITH FIRE AND A PIECE OF SILVER

how LA burned and justice lay clocked
upon
an intersection before that truck
got stuck,
I found myself alone. the church lot's
lines, white
lash marks on the newly laid blacktop—
night like
a riot of black people crossing
the church
driveway, asking me, torches, street lamps,
street lamps
like torches, the pitchfork trees, Hill Ave.'s
traffic,
—was it voices—asking me over
the starched
choir, indoors, toning, tromping through
that tune,
"O Lawd I Wanna Be A Christian
Inna
My Heart"—*are there white people inside?*
up high
the moon, silver coin, flips—heads, tails—and
again.

THE CITY VS. JOHN HENRY

1. DESTINY OF A STEEL DRIVING MAN

a natural man
driving steel in
the still of un
natural night   low
in the metro
below unnatural
dark the steel
hammer nail
the third rail
—all the little
blue blazes—he'll
die with his hammer
in his hand   yes lord
he'll

2. ...SKYSCRAPERS AND EVERYTHING

Mr J Hammer Henry
with your black
as rail spike neck
mallet muscled Mr J Bama
Henry outlantish from station
could barely fit   hammer
poking from stowage like
natural man's poke
to haymaker skyscrapers
to deep city sleep
sun red from smoke   weeping
say *don't go*
John Henry natural man
electric traffic light
raise its bloody hand
don't go
across that street

3. LOSING RELIGION

John get on track
you a bled in the wool Christian
ain't you   can't be seen crossing
this scarlet street

no valley to heaven
lay in quim nor bosom
you rail spike in dry loam
you good for working   dying

and where your hammer
ain't safe here for a myth
to travel without metonym   mis
understood despite your manhood

so hold it
just like steel
say

CLANG!
ain't that natural

4. IN THERAPY
dream every spike a nail driven
into America's hoof *gon ride this country*
down John say *to the ocean to drink*
up through the black mountains for a view
he see America's pinto hide stretched
over its sweatful bones galloping
toward City   unnatural as a stable
City say *where you think the train was going*

John John go
CLANG! CLANG!
and the train go

5 . IN A STATION AT THE METRO

first metrocard you bought
made your hammer bend but
your eyes lit   near electrical
your funk ain't wilt wan petals
at station   which still felt haunted
big negroes are expected   paid
for   but this here natural   John
once subway clanged tracks in
your grave   you were run through   steel
machine devouring the body
of some America   did that crimson
blood of yours feel yellow or green
get a move on John   go
even you shouldn't block the closing doors

6. OBITUARY

no one doubts your heart John
the busted meat of it   the machine
carve the right angles of your grave
raise high its robot arms   never alive
bury the never alive   let them   drop
                                    on down oh
                                    let them
                                    drop
                                    on down well now

and the robots go on
with what they call singing   sound
like digging for the dead or hammers
giving America a charlie horse
CLANG!ANG! let them   drop
CLANG!   on down oh
CLANG!   let them
                        drop
                        on down well now

every city here built of bones
blood   erupted flesh interred   the end
of the line John just like you pictured it
natural man death ain't the robots'
and every body here built of stone   let them   drop
                                        on down oh
                                        let them
                                        drop
                                        on down well now

CITY WITH FIRE AND A CHOIR AT REST

how LA burned as the people split
and dropped
to either side of a camcorder,
liquor
store, Desert Eagle, highway, siren.
I found
myself in the choir loft among
white men
and white women, sopranos, basses.
Jesus
leapt out nobody's mouth and I sat
to eat
the fistful of songs I was given.
April
sunset, the goddamned silence was fuel.

[IT] *don't want to be called your* { ✱ NIGGER ✱ }

it's best not to err and ER the A
if one must air the n_ _ _ _ _.
the ER is a looming heir
of that gloomy era where
n_ _ _ _ _s were in the air
in the best knots. IT knows that
to *catch a n_ _ _ _ _ by the toe*
is a way to pick the very best one.
when the n_ _ _ _ _ is to end up knotted
in the air, IT knows by your inheritance
IT is going to be IT. the A may still be
IT, but IT's ITS IT. see De Despair…

since that's ITS name,
wear IT out.

en✱eye*double guh*errrrr

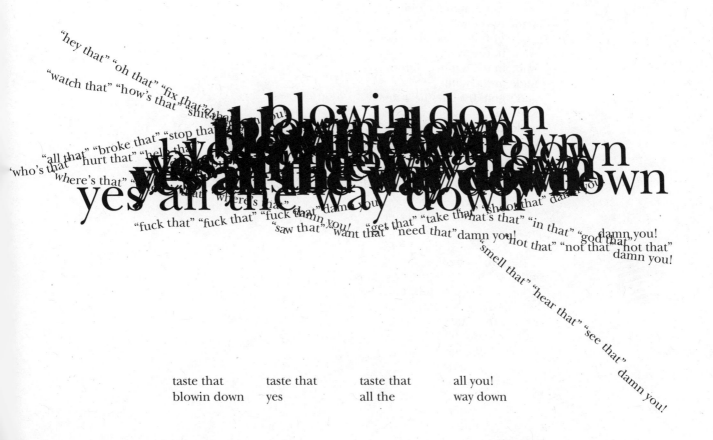

taste that   taste that   taste that   all you!
blowin down   yes   all the   way down

FLOODSONG 2: WATER MOCCASIN'S SPIRITUAL

wade in the water
wade in the water, children
wade in the water
god's gon' trouble the water
wade in the water
wade in the water, children
wade in the water
god's gon' trouble the water
wade in
wade in
wade in
              trouble
       in the water
          the water children
       in the water
              trouble the water
god's
                 children
       in the water
god's
                 children
      gon'
      in the water
             trouble
      in the water
             trouble
      in the water
             water
             water
             water
   god's gon

FLOODSONG 3: ALLIGATOR'S QUIET STORM

'Trina she my long leg woman.
my long leg woman she love me.
she love me and she pour the water.
she pour the water o my 'Trina.

'Trina she my hot blooded woman.
hot bloody: she love me!
she love me. sh'eat my kettle,
heat my kettle, o——my 'Trina!

'Trina she strong arm woeman.
stwrong woman, she love me!
love me and set the table.
uh set the table, o my 'Trina.

'Trina she my good hand woman—
my good hard woman. love me!
she love me and serve up suppers,
she serve me. o! my! 'Trina.

'Trina: she muh big eye wmmman,
me big eyed wooo, man! she love me!
she love me. she give me seconds.
give me seconds! o my

SWIMCHANT FOR NIGGER MER-FOLK
(AN AQUABOOGIE SET IN LAPIS)

never learned to swim/but me sho can di

O, VERMILION SHIP—D'WAH-WAH OOO.*v*
OVER MILLIONS SHIPPED. WAH-WAH-OO.*e*

let yo fishbone slip 'omen/let yo fishbone slip o men/

mako wish

ye black fish

mako feed

be black bleed .

they's comp'ny

comin comin

and all about was a darkening cloud and the gullets filled of brine and kine [cattle/chattel]

charnel channel of a deep blue. See

all about that darkening cloud and the gullets full of water and the gullets full of slaughter, [a salt/assault] *o*

charnel channel of a deep blue sea.

Poseidon slides his foaming shroud assured no one will see.

"jus look at de worl aroun you   right ere on de ocean floor   such wonduhful tings surroun you   what more is you lookin for?"

they's comp'ny haintin haintin/can't re-member; c'ant remember/

let yo fishbone slip 'omen/let yo fishbone slip o men

hammerheads'
hammers head
to ham (or head?)
'til hammers fed
o they's comp'ny
knockin knockin

grate white jaw
AW! great white
jaw-jaw juju
gnaw gnaw NO! NO...
they's comp'ny
dinin dinin

duppyguppies say
stay we in azure-amber
can't re-member;
c'ant remember
o they's comp'ny
haintin haintin

[so sang a pair of raggit claws/scuttlin cross the flo of silent seas. o, ye nigger mer-folk.
a lovesong fo songlubbers! it'll all be fin(e)???]

**ATTENTION: NIGGER MERMAIDS, MERMEN & MERNINNIES CHAINED LIKE HOOKED & SINKED SARDINNIES:
DO NOT BLEED IN THE SEA. THE STAINS WON'T WASH OUT. WE AIN'T'NT RESPONSIBLE FOR YOUR MESS.
MUCH OBILGED, THEE MANAGEMENT**
{Voyage: through.}

o they's comp'ny haintin haintin/the stains won't wash out

~~my~~ *name is...* }⟶ IT ain't from here; IT *is* here.
ITS
mud slurred through water.
mud made here to a here IT is. so
if there IT goes, here is gone, too
and IT will still be from nowhere
but here.

{ IT *ain't where* [IT's] *from*
{ IT's *where* [IT's] *at*

IT seeks asylum from a when
not a where. still, time
seeps in to place like lost family
portraits deep in mud, sepia into sepia.
tally poplar rings, every year a new spiral,
going back to mark a progress.

here is gone and took IT with it.

un- *derwater/-de- -de- -derwater*

to remove stains: rinse, repeat. *the stains won't wash out.*

*RE the *FU: *gee, what a surprise.

FLOTSAM

                          waterlogged mattress
                                rides the floodhead fitfully.
        gliding, August clouds.

                                                mosquito-spangled
                              dusk—debris sinking into
              high umber water.

                                      aluminum boats
              hew the still water, shovels
                                  shift dirt, cypress cones.

FLOODSONG 4: MOSQUITOES' DRINKING DITTY

drink ev'ry hour, next up this hour
and ev'ry hour after!
was born down in the river, there's
enough to go around!

drink ever ours, next on the hour
and ever ours after!
was brown din in the river, there is
nought to go aground!

drink ev'ry hour, neck-up the shower
and ne'er a shallow after!
was borne down by a river, theirs
enough to go around!

drink ev'ry hour nixed-up this our
and ever area rafter!
downpour upon the river, there
sea loves to go ground!

drink carry ours messed up the sour sand
devilry sow laughter!
were burned down by the river, err
enough to go around!

drink air is nixed, oar up the ebony
land is ere hereafter!
drowned morsels; bite the survivors—
go around they are enough!

FLOODSONG 5: BULLFROG'S LITURGY OF THE EUCHARIST

OFFERING

to each Below: the Above.
to each Out: the In.
to each Never: Ever.

CONSECRATION

by

     my heart of trembling mud,
     my blood of falling sand,
     my mind of teeming fens,
     my hands of moulding stones,
     my bones of melting song,
     my tongue of humming ghosts,
     my throat of burning eggs,
     my legs of diving wings,
     my lungs of rain:
        this ruin—
          too
        —is will.

COMMUNION

this flesh, serpent's.
this flesh, fish's.
this flesh, rodent's.

this skin is nowhere;
the insides, everywhere, out.

BENEDICTION

go home, though it is death:
at home, you shall find your service.

this—too—is will.

FLOODSONG 6: GULL'S MADSONG

ocean is a-coming in,
loudly sang the walker.
      the pouring wind!
      the tearing rain!
and roofs beneath the river.

sang walker!

fishes in the cradle!
babies in the stew!
      "if I had wings,
      or just one wish,
I'd climb the air with you!"

  walker, walker!
how sang he, sang he!
how he sang, he sang!

FLOODSONG 7: CATFISH'S BOUNCE

I've known.   I've known.   I've known. I've– . I've– .
    I've known.   I've known. I've– . I've– .
I've known.   I've known.   I've known. I've– . I've– . I've known
garbage.   muddy. and it went
            down. to sleep.

I heard.   . I heard.   I heard. I– . I– .
    I heard.   I heard. I– . I– .
I heard.   I heard.   I heard. I– . I– . I heard
singing.   dusky. of the miss-
         ing. I've seen.

I've known.   I've known.   I've known. I've– . I've– .
    I've known.   I've known. I've– . I've– .
I've known.   I've known.   I've known. I've– . I've– . I've known

y'all

FLOODSONG 8: STRAYED DOG'S CALL &

: the every I learned
                          : ...
         : food
for the good. love
                          : ...
         : your hand
smiled with meat. you
wanted me
to understand you with
                          : ...
       : my teeth.
hunger seemed the only
                          : ...
       : tongue
we shared.
the sky
            : ...
    : opened, closed
its door. the sky
                        : ...
      : opens, closes
its door. the sky —

hunger, seems the only. master,
know we both understand
something like love. "good
doggy good doggy" what I do now.

(in the cut)

it's like that
   and that's the way IT *is.*

IT is just like it isn't IT?

breaking mirrors is black cats
whutting the why of it.

what ←

is a…if IT *ain't*
   got a gun?

the how of whut is to cast
the it IT is like to just like it is. *i.e.*

IT *ain't nothing, really.*

the whut of IT is why
black cats is broken mirrors.

IT isn't IT: just like it is.

}

what IT *do,*
baby?

so sun down to sun up/run up with [ITS] *gun up*

                     …/all day. e'ey day.

CITY OF SEARCHLIGHTS AND DEAD CATS

blocks below us, the searchlights
bend, street lines into descent—

the Ghetto Bird makes its vulture round—
a muzzle flash up and down

somewhere a block away, someone breaks,
running for a ride. the cops roll up

and down the blocks below us.
we bend into descent.

AND WHAT TO CALL THE HOMIE NOW,
the name I cried at the ivy whip—

leaves the shape of vipers' skulls
leaves his hands stripped—no longer fits.

don't play up in that ivy, y'all
there're snakes in all the vines. the lines

of his name became the drawl of red aerosol.
a language you taught me. a bullet makes

a mouth in a heart, a toothless mouth. the bones
a handful of dominoes.

call him "Buph Lōc," nigga, the mouth says,
at once a tilted 40.

FEVER! THE BONES BURIED IN THE CARD TABLE. I
empty my wallet of cusswords. *domino!*

I can't seem to beat you. I hold my bones,
their dull eyes gawking black at me.

Dallas!
brother!

you stared down a coyote.
you snuck home a kitten.

I am letting my bones drop,
a wall unbuilding. I stare

at each eye, slowly counting.
you know, now, I walk every street

I ever walk knowing how I'd kill
everyone I've come across?

and when I look at you, I am gawking back
at me, needing new eyes.

AND WHEN I LOOKED AT MY BOYS,
they became a gang just as 1-time

suspected. and when my boys turned on me,
school was a mess of ivy.

those nights, coyotes in scared packs
upset cans to get at the sacks

of cold cuts gone bad, take-home chicken bones.
those nights, I ran ammonia over the remains,

those sour nights sliced by copter blades.
the possums and their buckshot eyes

taught us to lay dead, as suspected.
my name X'd off the walls; still

my posse never fought
me. we were coyotes at heart.

they became Grimace, Dimen', Inches, Goldy:
for his skin, his hope. that was then,

I don't call them now. I don't know

WHAT HAPPENED? POPS WOULDN'T SAY.
I drive home, my headlights

break against big coyotes ambling
toward a fence. bold now,

swole from eating cats; upright trash
cans line the drives like families

awaiting those inevitable hearses. I drag
the garbage, clutch an ax handle,

trundle past where Pops found her,
mangled, the cat you brought home years ago

without permission. a muzzle flashes up
and down somewhere a block away

a coyote fills its mouth with red aerosol
and swaggers up the street.

the searchlights hit it,
new eyes glare back.

THE CRUEL, CRUEL CITY

cruel, cruel city, that Stetson. all stank-eye gaslight; bodying
row house; blue nigger rag. unborn bullet trains
express from the broke-windowed convenience stores
of *Gonna* to the musty, unlit flops of *I Did;* ever
on time like nothing else. you wide-brimmed tenement;
mothballed and boxed alley dead ending;
light blocking: cruel, cruel Stetson.

when the songs pour over dark guitars,
those wounds of sound, heavy, jangled, the Stetson
is like a woman, prize for two tore-back pimps, neither's bottom,
but new booty hoodoo, stakes for a hand of spades.
when the macks slash the song out of air, Billy Lyons
lying at the end of a barstool, as though a pistol said: *roll
over!* tame-ass Billy, reclined in the Bucket of Blood, bleeding pale,
emptied like he was full of dirty water. Billy the Lion
just now releasing the jacked Stetson hat and Stag's new brown suit.

there weren't no new brown suit. the running red running out
William de Lyons from a different jig of monkey
and pawn shop—back to stank-eye
gaslight, back to bodying row house, back rag nigger blue.
                              —*wanksta-ass poet, them whiteboys made a ape outta—*

the gangstered Stetson
                    hollered to its revolver lover. (people don't kill
niggers, niggers kill niggers) *and of course you realize,*

it's a white man's world a white lady from church once whispered to me,
like I ain't know people don't kill monkeys, monkeys
kill monkeys. cruel and cruel city, nigger manhood
—rather, that damned hat, thus passed betwixt a lion
and a riverboat, and bloody ditty doo-wah,
structured row of doo wop gennimens and afflicted ballet of diddy
bop thugs to this wanksta-ass poet who can now:

1) eat a ton of dog shit without getting sick.
2) dance underwater and not get wet.
3) fuck hot pussy until it's cold. or

fortify that old time vita.

you know how Douglas do. you do know how D do!

next week, I'll stand, damned hat—rather, manhood in hand
like a cover letter (... do ... he do) in those washed offices, declaring:

"I should like to publish in your little magazine."

RwanDun moaning radio *no, no, no, no, no…*
Raw & da hits keep comin raw
& da club bangers keep it rah-rah …*yeah, yeah, yeah, yeah, yeah.*

let me see that tootsee roll!

(O)O.G.s figure subtraction eradicates
difference. they sun-up to sun-down—
someone must be picked.

…[IT's] *been rewired to work*   *you don't know…*
punks run when [IT] *put in work*   *your brother…*
niggas on the block, man they got that work   *…you hate the most*

…*not work* …/*ludicrous*

IT wasn't there at the time;
but IT's from a long line of workers,
thus remains inclined to work out
problems, suh.

[IT's] *not a problem that* [IT] *can't fix.*
no sweat.

(goin' back)

ERIC VISITS MR. BUTLER'S

new carport, Thursday, 2:00, there's Eric bent
like a manicurist at his retired father's

classic roadster. hands that roughed JC pigskin
before gliding crow-like over clean-room beakers

grip dripping rags. the check
he won as settlement? long since gone.

Eric stares at the passenger door
like his reflection is a stain. he is

unsure whether *wrongful termination*
is a blot or badge. Sheriff's Department

jobs demand good credit; Eric's children
have eaten the calendar. so when

he said: *please, I can do this, let me try.*
I want to support my family,

and that his face was a wet rag, you know
the officers stared, unsure.

up from the door, hands empty and wet, he takes
a towel, dries that shiny white car's dark windshield.

empties the wash water in the lawn he just mowed,
happy, perhaps, to feed something.

RECYCLING THE CITY

was a time I would eat anything
torn from my body, as a city
recycles its bricks after trauma.
so I would eat the bitter black things,
those brittle wound stones. was a time, torn,
I'd eat anything from my body,
those yellowed bark ridges. a city
recycles gypsum after trauma.
I'd eat anything, pale crescents torn,
those Moor-less swords. after, a city
recycles. green things from my body,
those rotting gems. those sour gray things—
wasted clay. city, after trauma,
recycles its iron, those bones torn
from a city as though—a body:
those swords and bones, gypsum, gems. trauma:
a torn time recycled. a body
as a city, torn into a thing.

THE SIX CITIES

I. CITY

ladies and gentlemen: the city of blocks.
—city blocks, not children's—one letter
at a time we learn words are walls,
houses, bridges; but that's children's. city blocks,
one letter at a time we learn words can stain.
blight is a word. as is *tag* but not children's
games. the blood in the city wells. ladies
and gentlemen: the city of letters.
we plan words one letter at a time. we stain
cities well. tag! not children's games;
lessons. if at first you don't succeed: ladies
and gentlemens, the city of childrens. not
the blocks. gentleman, lady: we
learn words, well, unwell:— m o r p h o l o g y p r o b l e m s
one letter at a time—
                            like children? yes.
                                          please.

II. CITY

yesterday, I woke and believed I was a city, a green one.

but the city fell away like a gray robe of taxis and neon,
of mannequins and manholes. sweetheart, let's go down to the water,

yes, though not the water of what we don't want. rather

that river we remember flowing from the thick, damp under-
brush. a place we've wished to visit, both of us. now, let's really go.

we'll follow the water like a child learning to walk shadows

its parents, both wearing green jackets as though the wind
tells them: *teach your child that people can be places, can be coppices,*

can be groves, a stand of trees. and I learned this. I've been so many places

in my life; once, perhaps a city with emerald colonnades and spires
like a thousand jackets hung on steeple-backed chairs.

but that wasn't it. I was a forest whose roots hadn't destroyed

a green city but had tasted it into themselves, even as I did,
when I found myself at the mouth of the place you are called *river.*

and when I drank to be changed, I became a gully. right there,

in the hollow below the city that was not there at all—
but distant, like a place in a brochure. still, we had become several

rushes, so to dream of paper would be to dream of children un-becoming—no,

I am *riverbank*, silt pulled slowly back into the current, where the salmon,
weary in its crimson envelope, says: *children are a place; drift too long*

they will be behind you. you look at me to name the place we become.

III. CITY

city of pavement groves
and cement plots,
tarmac gardens
and cinderblock vineyards,
concrete fields,
plaster orchards
and asphalt patches:
—antagonist.

IV. CITY

and we opened each locked gate
in the crowded city. we knew how,
what to do. we broke down
the city's walls. they fell out.
all the children we had been
waiting for. each we looked at
more beautiful than the last,
the last more beautiful than—
and knowing the one we chose
would be the child to live,
weren't we proud? our eyes
broken with such smiling,
didn't they just weep pink, blue?

V. CITY

the city of black cohosh.
the city of arginine.
the city of red clover blossoms.
the city of zinc—zinc and copper.
the city of tribulus and saw palmetto.
the city of selenium, l-carnitine.
the city of gotu, of gotu kola.
what to do. what to-do.

VI. CITY

in the city of dented infants
to-be, the clocks have all stopped.
the eyes' tears, geometric and foul. dirty
tractor-trailers lumber up, urgent—
the skid marks, the shards and fluid
—with crooked cargo. keep reversing
into fire hydrants. keep humping
over the curb. porch lights missing
every doormat. kitchen doorway's warped—
in, out, out, in, my woman, stirring her empty
iron pot. the bottom of all things, dry-
snake-in-a-drained-well-like. fucking
fire—below that *great* obelisk—
knocking its broken neck against the smoke.

NOTES

THE BLACK AUTOMATON IN *TAG*

uses Young Jeezy, "Go Getta" and Monie Love, "Monie in the Middle."

THE BLACK AUTOMATON IN DE DESPAIR UB EXISTENCE #3: HOW CAN I BE DOWN?

uses Speech (Arrested Development), "Tennessee"; Kool Keith (Ultramagnetic MCS), "Ego Trippin'" via Black Thought (The Roots), "Concerto of the Desperado"; and Biv (BBD), "Poison."

THE VOLTRON COMMUNIQUÉS

features Voltron III (Golion) a kick-ass anime robot composed of five lion-shaped space crafts. The Black Lion is housed on a pedestal near the "Lion Castle"; the Blue Lion, in a lake; the Yellow Lion in a desert cave; the Red Lion, beneath a volcano; and the Green Lion, in a huge tree in the woods. This poem is dedicated to Pam Noles, Bao Phi and K. D. Stewart.

"SPIT OUT ALL BITTERNESS"

was stretched over a partial skeleton of David Wagoner's "Staying Alive."

THE BLACK AUTOMATON IN WHAT IT IS #2: HYPERTENSION IN EFFIZZECT

uses Skee-Lo, "I Wish"; Boss, "Deep"; Ice Cube, "The Nigga Ya Love to Hate"; Scarface (Geto Boys), "My Mind Playin Tricks on Me"; Mos Def, "Got"; Nas, "NY State of Mind"; Threat, "Nowhere to Hide"; and Common, "The Corner."

THE BLACK AUTOMATON IN DE DESPAIR UB EXISTENCE #1: UP YE MIGHTY RACE!!!

uses Dr. Dre/Parliament, "Let Me Ride"/"The Mothership Connection"; Goodie Mob, "Cell Therapy"; Melle Mel (Grandmaster Flash & the Furious 5), "The Message"; and Redman & Method Man/Silver Convention, "How High?"/"Fly Robin Fly."

THE BLACK AUTOMATON IN WHAT IT IS #1: GETTING OF THE POT

uses Jay-Z, "Money Ain't a Thing"; KRS-One (BDP), "My Philosophy"; Talib Kweli, "Good to You"; Professor X (X Clan); and Snoop Doggy Dogg, "Gin and Juice."

THE CITY VS. JOHN HENRY

follows the famous folk hero who competed against a mechanical steam drill in a railroad challenge. He died with his hammer in his hand. "Skyscrapers and everything" is from Stevie Wonder's "Living for the City."

THE BLACK AUTOMATON IN *TAG*

uses Flavor Flav (Public Enemy), "Yo Nigga" and DMX.

SWIMCHANT FOR NIGGER MER-FOLK

uses Parliament, "Aquaboogie (Psychoalphadiscobetabioaquadooloop)"; Sebastian (from *The Little Mermaid*), "Under the Sea"; then snaps up Eliot and shanghais Hayden. A mako is a kind of shark. A duppy is a murder victim's ghost.

THE BLACK AUTOMATON IN *TAG*

uses Eminem, "My Name Is"; Rakim (Eric B & Rakim), "I Know You Got Soul"; and Digital Underground, "Underwater Rhymes."

FLOODSONG 7: CATFISH'S BOUNCE

was composed in an attempt to synthesize Bounce tracks. "Bounce" is a music style with roots in New Orleans. This poem scavenges from Hughes.

THE BLACK AUTOMATON IN DE DESPAIR UB EXISTENCE #2: OUR NEW DAY BEGUN

uses Run DMC, "It's Like That"; Q-Tip (A Tribe Called Quest), "What?!"; Paul Wall, "Grillz"; Prodigy (Mobb Deep), "Shook Ones Part 2"; Mack 10, "Hoo Bangin' (WSCG Style)"; and Peaches (featured with Outkast), "Peaches Intro."

CITY OF SEARCHLIGHTS AND DEAD CATS

is for my brother, Dallas.

THE CRUEL, CRUEL CITY

was written using the "20 Little Poetry Projects" exercise; thanks to Richard Garcia. It also alludes to "Run, Red, Run" as sung by The Coasters (penned by Lieber and Stoller). It uses Parliament, "Aquaboogie (Psychoalphadiscobetabioaquadooloop)"; Redman, "Soopa Man Luvva (Part 3)"; and AMG, "Bitch Betta Have My Money."

THE BLACK AUTOMATON IN WHAT IT IS #3: WORK IT OUT

uses Destiny's Child, "No, No, No, No, No"; The 69 Boys, "Tootsee Roll"; Posdnuos (De La Soul), "The Grind Date"; Ice Cube, "Wrong Nigga to Fuck Wit"; Ludacris, "Saturday (Ooo Ooo)"; Kool Moe Dee, "I Go to Work"; and Aceyalone (Haiku D'Etat), "Haiku D'Etat." Aceyalone is actually paraphrasing a line from Indeep's "Last Night a DJ Saved My Life," penned by Michael Cleveland. The poem conscripts Levine. Also, "Rwandan Hutus called mass slaughter 'the work.'"
—Donald G. Dutton, *The Psychology of Genocide, Massacres and Extreme Violence*

ERIC VISITS MR. BUTLER'S

is for Eric Butler.

THE SIX CITIES

has an epigraph from Jan Beatty's "Dear Mother, Machine."

ACKNOWLEDGMENTS

Heartfelt thanks to the editors of the following publications and websites in which versions of some of these poems appear: *Black Nature Poetry, cavecanempoets.org, chaparralpoetry.net, Eclipse, Ecotone, exittheapple.com, Fence, Gulf Coast, The Literary Review, miPoesias.com, Model Homes, Ninth Letter, Solo Cafe, Washington Square* and *The Yale Anthology of Younger American Poets.*

Thanks as well to the Callaloo Creative Writers' Workshop and the Idyllwild Summer Poetry Program where some of these poems were written and to the University at Albany and the New York State Writers Institute for their continuing support of Fence Books.

Also, overflowing helpings of thanks to the Poetry Society of America, the Mrs. Giles Whiting Foundation and, of course, Stephanie Stio, the National Poetry Series and its generous funders for all their heroic support. Great thanks to Catherine Wagner for saying: "This one!" and Rebecca Wolff for saying: "Fantastic!"

I am *deeply* grateful to my wife, Nicole, for sending me back to the drawing board; Jericho Brown, Yona Harvey, Jen Hofer, Amaud Johnson and K. D. Stewart for their judicious suggestions since.

To my family and friends, teachers, students and colleagues—I left folks out last time so I won't risk it this time—just thanks. All of you.

Finally, like a boxer whom has just broken an opponent's face, I thank God.

ABOUT THE AUTHOR

Poet/performer/librettist Douglas Kearney's first full-length collection of poems, *Fear, Some*, was published in 2006 by Red Hen Press. In 2008, he was honored with a Whiting Writers' Award and in 2007, the Poetry Society of America named him a notable New American Poet. Born in Brooklyn, raised in Altadena and now living with his family in California's San Fernando Valley, he earned a BA from Howard University, an MFA in Writing from the California Institute of the Arts (where he now teaches) and held fellowships with Cave Canem, Callaloo and Idyllwild. Visit him online at www.douglaskearney.com.